Also by Frederick Franck:

Days with Albert Schweitzer 1959

My Friend in Africa 1960

African Sketchbook 1961

My Eye is in Love 1963

Outsider in the Vatican 1965

I love Life 1967

Exploding Church 1968

Simenon's Paris 1970

The Zen of Seeing 1973

Pilgrimage to Now/Here 1973

An Encounter with Oomoto 1975

The Book of Angelus Silesius 1976

Zen and Zen Classics 1977

Every One, the timeless myth of Everyman Reborn 1978

The Awakened Eye 1979

Art as a Way 1981

The Supreme Koan 1982

The Buddha Eye 1982

READERS:

Au Pays du Soleil 1958

Au Fil de l'Eau 1964

Croquis Parisiens 1969

Tutte le strade portano a Roma 1970

Bottomless well
from which all rises, grows
and boundless Ocean
back into which it flows

Angelus Silesius, 17th Century

The water that boils in the kettle
is drawn from the Well
that is bottomless

Sen Rikyu, 14th Century Tea Master

Thou art the deepest well,
the millennia never tired
drinking from thee

Li Tai Pe, 7th Century, on the Tao

VINTAGE BOOKS · A DIVISION OF RANDOM HOUSE · NEW YORK

Echoes from the Bottomless Well

as heard by

Frederick Franck

A Vintage Original March 1985

First Edition

 Published in the United States by Random House, Inc., New York, and simultaneously in Canada by Random House of Canada Limited, Toronto

Library of Congress Cataloging in Publication Data:

Franck, Frederick 1909-

Echoes from the bottomless Well

1. Philosophy, Oriental _ Quotations, maxims, etc.

I. Title

B 121. F7 1985 181 84-20855

ISBN 0-394-72995-1

Manufactured in the United States of America

This book is dedicated to the Sages and Poets quoted here from memory and according to my understanding, and to those whose translations made them accessible.

It started just before Easter. I had received a letter from a woman I had known since 1939, when I lived in England. I had seen her only twice since then; once some thirty years ago, and another time when we had lunch in London, perhaps fifteen years later.

Meanwhile our friendship continued by transatlantic airmail. At times I found this stream of letters burdensome, an extra duty... one has so many duties. I would postpone my reply a few weeks, until her next letter arrived and made me feel guilty. Often I thought of breaking the habit, but then I knew how lonely her life had become and how poor she was. One wondered how she could afford the airmail stamps.

In this latest letter she wrote: "I have not been at all well lately... Yesterday I sat in my chair without moving —I must have looked like a Madame Tussaud wax figure— but these little attacks kept coming... It makes one think, and it makes one face reality at depth, which is the only place where it lies. What can separate me from the love of Christ, the Reality within? I hope nothing will separate me from it now. It is the truth of one's being. And if it is mixed up with 'God' — O.K.! For it IS God — my self — Itself, and therefore inextinguishible. Reality IS!..."

Was this a leave taking? A last farewell?

I sat in my studio, shaken, much more so than I would have believed possible. I scribbled a note to her: "See a cardiologist at once, a good one! Send me the bill...." I would mail it immediately after the Easter weekend.

I was not sure what to do next.

On the table in front of me, in a jam jar full of pencils, pipe cleaners, scissors, stood two brushes I once bought in Kyoto — an ordinary Japanese writing brush and a little flat square one which had just taken my fancy. I don't know really why I bought them. I had never used them: I am not an Oriental, and where I come from one draws with a pen or a pencil.

There are always some bottles of India ink in various solutions on my table, and before I knew what was happening, I had taken a sketchpad and with the little square brush... No! I must have used the writing brush first to make that dot...a dot that looked like a water drop—and yet was a portrait...A self portrait? A portrait of my friend who was now dying?

Then came another dot, and another, and another. Each was a person I knew, each the center of a circle of which the invisible circumferences intersected... On the next sheet the drops appeared again, more faintly this time, and around them the square brush traced the infinite circumference that embraced them all, the Ocean in which all we waterdrops merge, water to water...

From then on the drawings—if these metaphysical doodles are drawings—kept erupting on the paper, one after the other, in an unstoppable stream, and in a style different from anything I had ever done before. My hand seemed to move automatically, obeying some irresistible impulse. It was as if, on a screen in front of me, an image appeared that had fused with a poem, a saying, a koan, welling up from nowhere, and transcribing itself, without my interference onto the paper.

I say "as if from nowhere", for these Siamese twins of word and image seemed to rise from such depths of memory that it felt as if my own recollections were echoes from the bottomless well of our collective human memory.

There was no time to think, even less to worry whether the quotations were literally correct and properly attributed to a Rinzai, a Saint John, a Bashō: the signatures on the screen were often indistinct. But that did not seem to matter at all, for I was simply recording what had over all these years become mine, or perhaps I had become it — It!

In no-time, in a few quick strokes, the brush traced what appeared on the screen of the inner eye, while the inner ear listened... This continued all day and deep into the night. Then I slept for a few hours and when I woke up, I was sure I had dreamt it all.

But there was the floor strewn with sheets of paper! There was no time to look them over, for the moment I sat down the well began to echo again. I still remember Rinzai looking up from the floor, as he told his monks about the "True Man without rank or label in this mass of red flesh" and shouting "Speak! Speak!!" at the one who dared ask for an explanation; and lying next to him, this time in human form, my self portrait, naked and seen from the back, wielding a brush in mute response to this "Speak! Speak!!"

It was puzzling and not a little frightening, this drugless high, in which the hand kept moving in calm frenzy. Once more it continued until nightfall. Then, suddenly, it stopped. I had run out of paper...

I began, dead tired as I was, to count the sheets. There were a hundred forty four of them—some soft feathery, some violent like a whiplash, others again smoothly flowing, stern or funny, but all freely brushed in a flash of impulse and each one showing something the words alone had left unsaid; each one a solution to a problem lost from sight.

As I started to sort through the sheets, a sequence appeared as inexplicably, as inexorably as did the twins of word and image themselves.

On Easter Monday the news came that Gerrie had died... Was what my hand precipitated on those sheets of paper her Requiem?

For years I had thought of gathering together crucial sayings, short texts, aphorisms, important enough to form a kind of layman's breviary, to take along to the uninhabited island, the prison cell, or any place where one could take at most one small book as a companion on the Way — through the falling darkness of this menacing age... I cannot help feeling that the Clear Light of my friend's final vision — she died immediately after mailing her letter — acted in some way as the catalyst which determined the form my "breviary" was to assume so suddenly: that of a Book of Hours, of Forty Eight Hours — not counting the preceding half a century...

The Requiem had become a celebration of Life.

frederick franck

Echoes from the Bottomless Well

. . . each dot : the center of a circle without circumference . . .

I know not what I am
but what I know I'm not
a thing, yet a no-thing
a circle, yet a dot. Angelus Silesius.

... the dots are still there, these water drops, but oh, so faintly...

Rinzai said:

"There is that True Man, without rank or label in this mass of red flesh... He goes in and out of your sense gates incessantly... Have you seen this True Man?"

"But, Master, what is that True Man?.."

Speak! Speak!

Rinzai Roku

Speak!

Speak!!

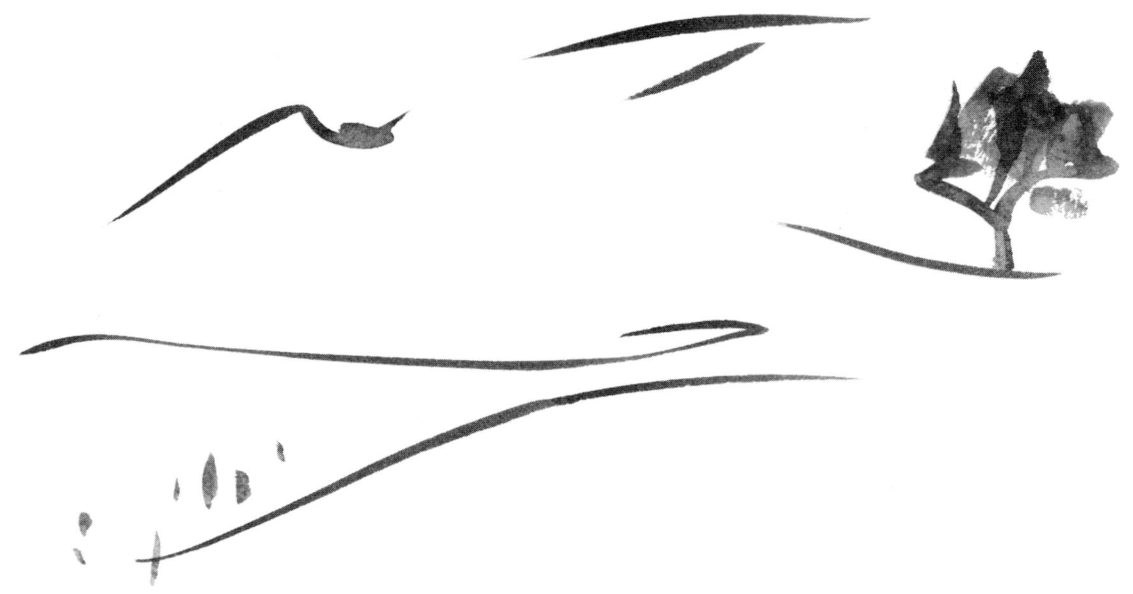

The landscape you draw
is an internal landscape
emerging from the
formless, colorless
Ground of Being

not Knowing
the
TRUE SELF,

○

the painter
draws his pictures
by
It

Lankavatara Sutra

"Is there anything more miraculous than the wonders of nature?" the monk asked. The Master answered: "Yes! Your awareness, Your understanding of the wonders of nature."

as the light of the Reality
of a thing flashes
fix it instantly
in your poem
before it fades out!

Bashō

a single leaf falling...
autumn is everywhere

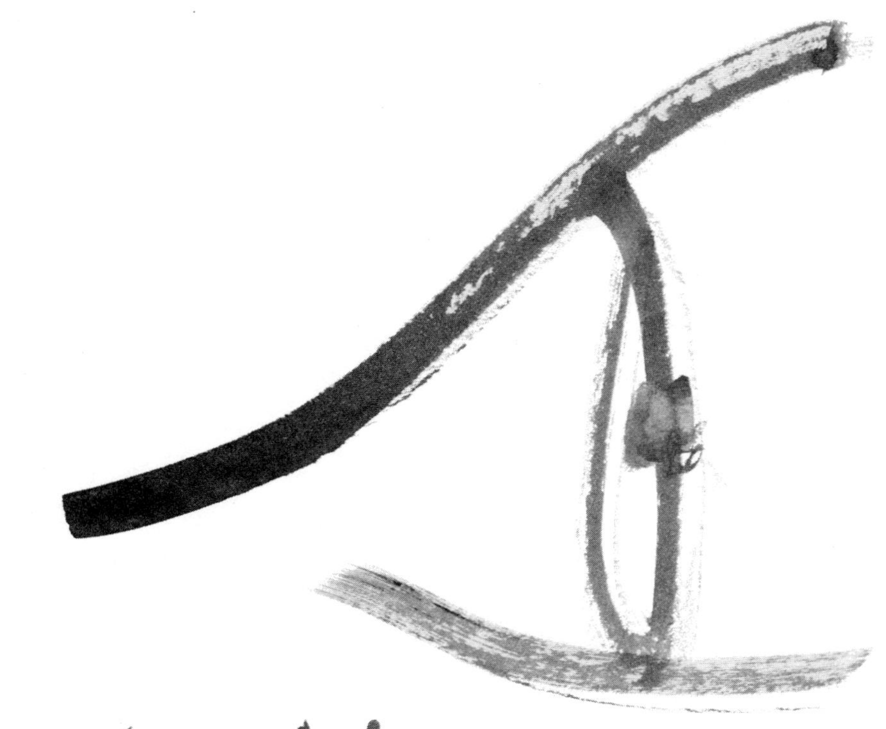

The Meaning
of Life
is to See!

Hui Neng

"I approve
of your seeing,"
the master said,

"so I am not worried
about what you do!"

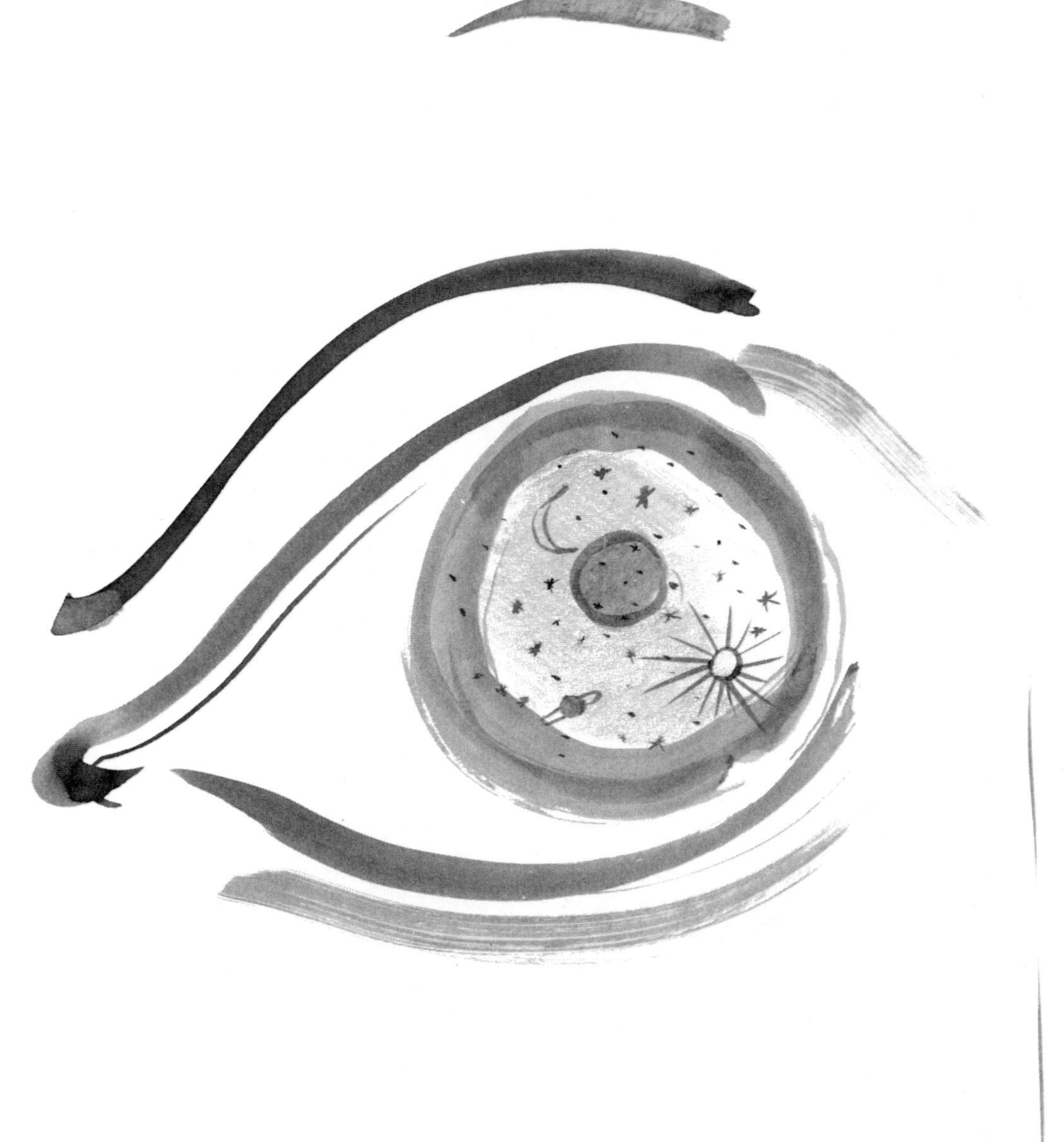

all this Universe
is in this eye
of mine!

Seppo

Monks should do their zazen in their zendo
I, a knight, practice it on horseback

Kamakura Koen

how wondrous!
I carry firewood!
I draw water!

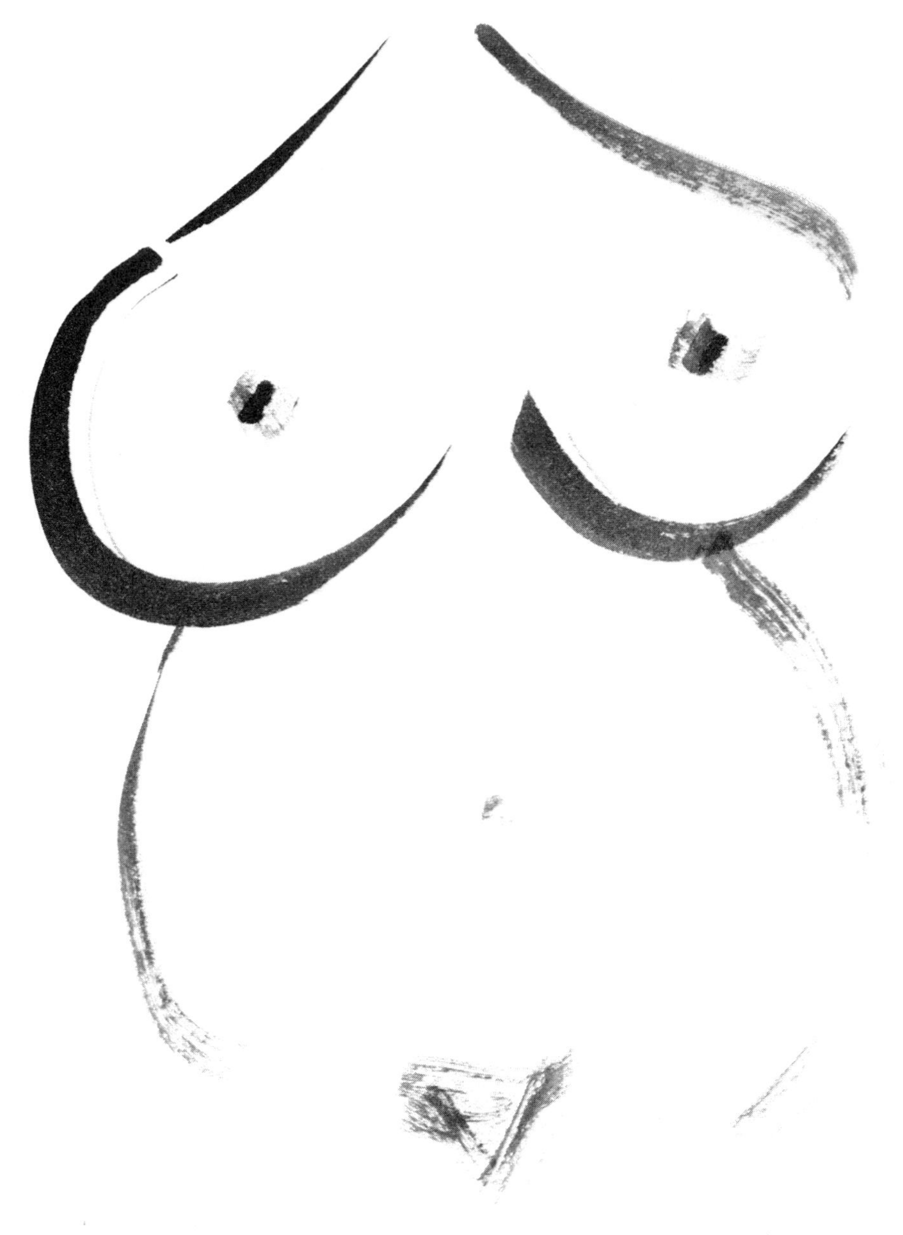

illusion is
the mantle
of the Real

The Mystical is not
the how of the
world
but that it exists

Wittgenstein

as to the skin
what a difference
between man and woman
but as to the bones
both so human!
Ikkyu

from here all the Buddhas
all the Christs
entered the World
The nun Myokei

All the sins
committed
in the three worlds
will fade away
together with myself

Ikkyu

the sinner's ego is crude
that of the saint refined,
distilled. Careful! It may
be more poisonous!

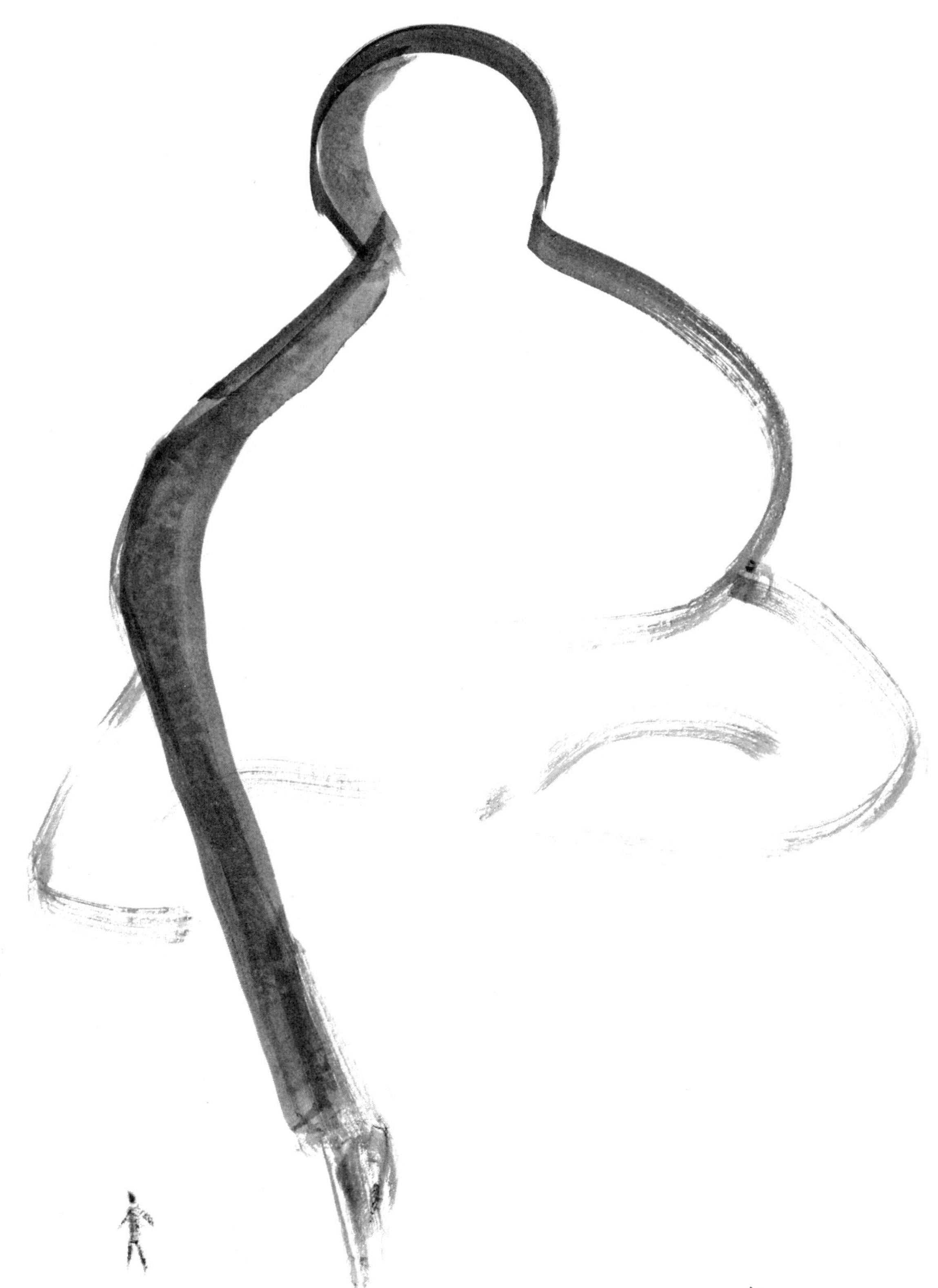

When a monk complained about the world's evil, the Buddha stretched his hand towards the Earth: "On this Earth I attained Liberation."

My short span of spring
how many years will it be?
Hanshan

Born like a dream
in this dream
of a world,
I who will fade
like the morning
dew

Ikkyu

Who is that "I"
that is speaking?

Ramana Maharshi

I am neither I
nor Other,
both I and other...

"You used to say: 'Mind is the Buddha.' Why do you say now:
'No Mind, no Buddha'?"
The Master answered: "I said 'Mind is the Buddha' to stop the baby crying."
"And when the baby stopped crying?"
"No mind no Buddha!"

Matsu

How old are you?

- As old as the Buddha.

And how old is the Buddha?

- As old as I am

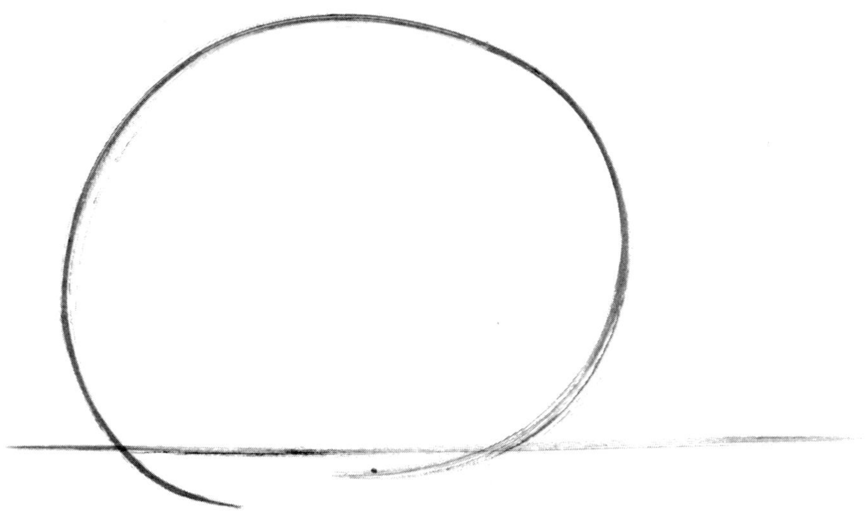

all at once
I saw
that the sun
was round!

Since then
I have been the happiest man on earth!

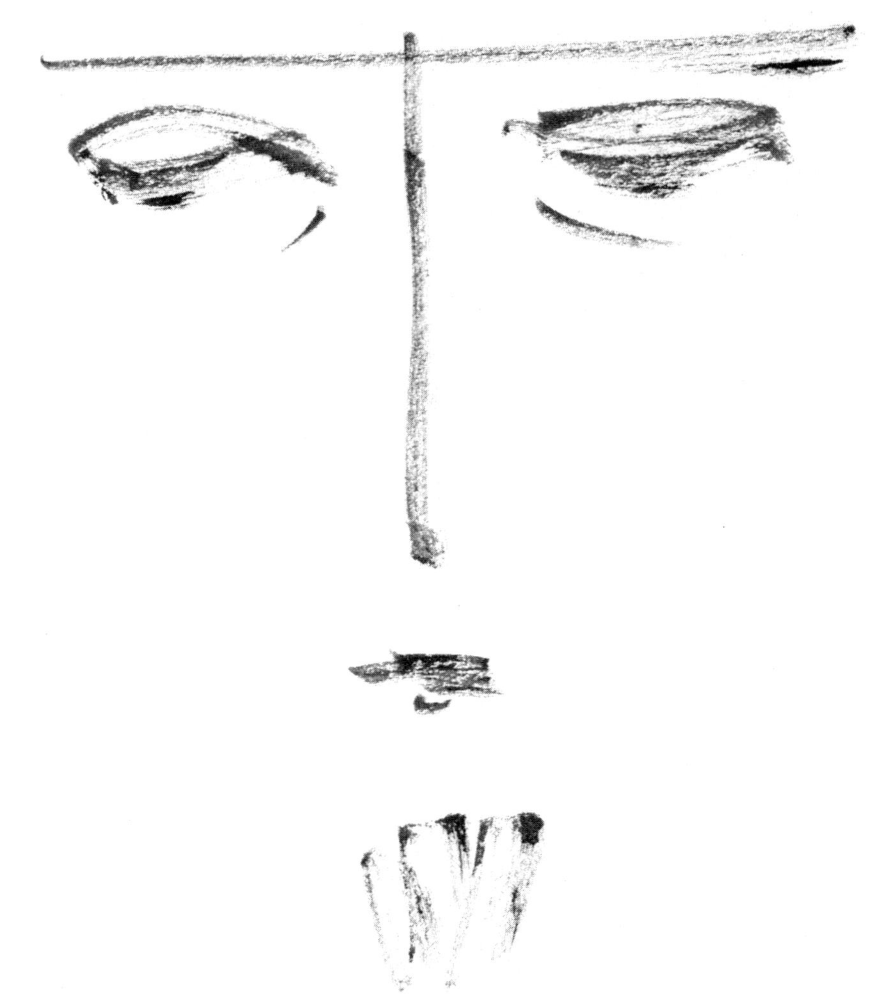

the eyes are horizontal
the nose... vertical

Dogen

the infinitely small is as large as the infinitely big.
Sengtsen

One thing

is all things

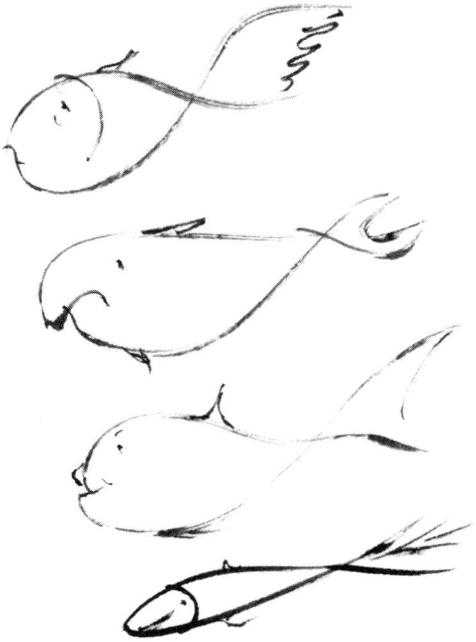

all things
are one
thing

yet, no thing
is a Thing

Hsin hsin Ming

When we speak of things
as they truly are
in themselves
we are in the field
of religion
Nishitani Keiji

It is like being immersed in the great ocean, the waves over your head, yet begging pitifully for water

gensha

the One embodies itself in the multitude of things; does not stand aloof from them

D.T. Suzuki

the Ten Thousand things and myself are of one root
Zazenron

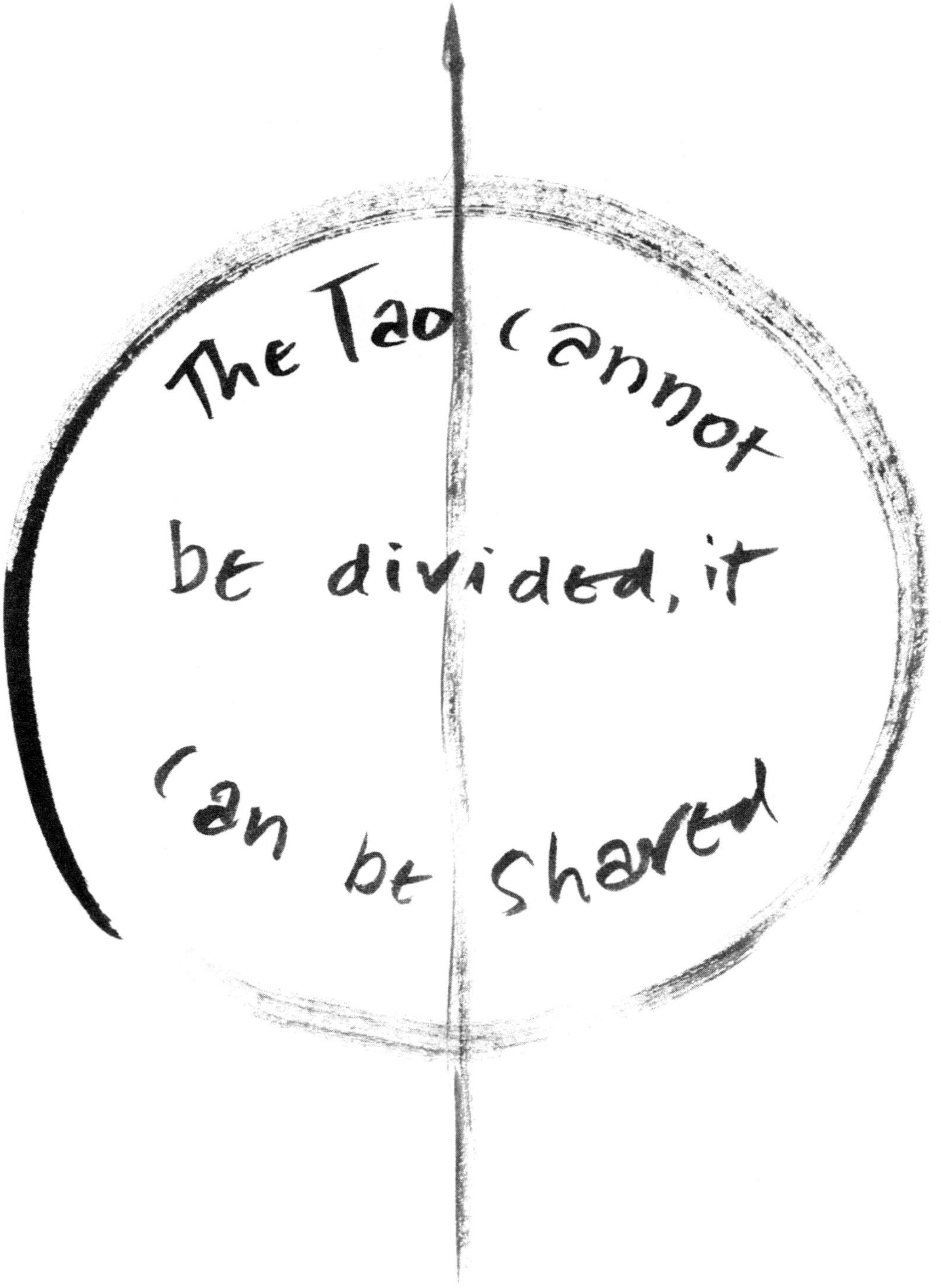

The Tao cannot
be divided, it
can be shared

the clearsighted eye turns the light back
to see its own Original Nature ...

Why do they call me a fool?
I wonder...
But how could I know
who doesn't even know
Who I is!

Hanshan

"What are you?"

– I am no What!

– I am only I . . .

in relation to you!

In all faces
is seen
the Face of Faces
veiled
as in a mirror

Nicholas of Cusa

Show me your Original Face
before you were born!
– Before Abraham was I AM!

Our Original Nature
from the beginningless past
is the same for all beings,
so it is called
the Buddha Nature
Daikaku

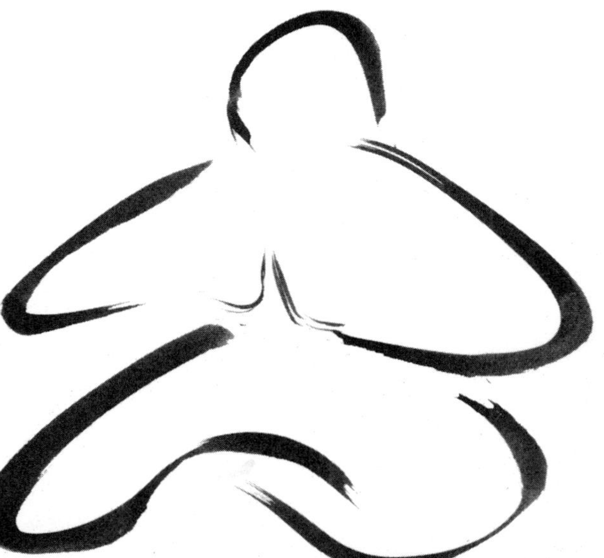

One deluded thought
and you are a common fellow,
one enlightened one
and you are a Buddha... Hui Neng

The more you look for it, the less you'll find it...

Yoka

...you can only BECOME it...

Ikkyu

the Buddha Mind
is one
with my own Essence

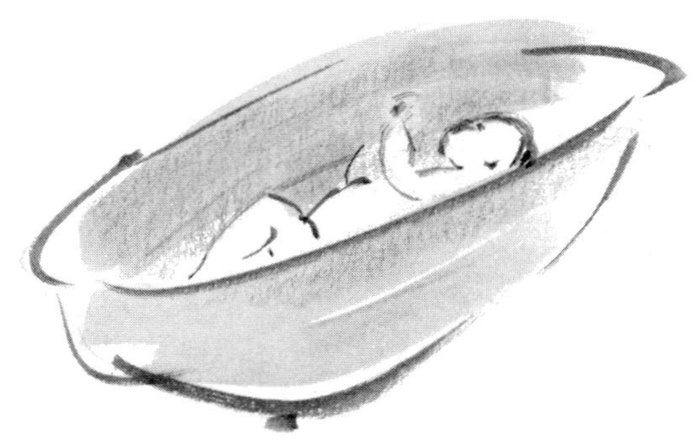

...there is the Unborn,
the Unconditioned
without which
no liberation
from the born,
the conditioned
could be attained...

the Buddha

I meet him
he is no other than myself
yet I am not him..

Dosan

the perfect man
uses his mind
as a mirror
It grasps nothing
It rejects nothing
It receives but
does not keep.

Chuang Tzu

as night falls, no more reflections
in the mirror
yet in this heart they are seen,
darkly...

Shotaku

All beings are the Buddha Nature

Emptiness, Sunyata, Nothingness
is the interdependent arising of
all existences — Nagarjuna

"Cut me a first-rate slice of meat"
the customer asked

"Is not everything I could slice here
first-rate?", the butcher answered.

does the dog
have the Buddha Nature?

Joshu

is there Buddha Nature
in the dog?

is the dog in the Buddha Nature?

You
call it
a
dog!

standing,
going
sitting.
whatever you have to do
and you are in the best place
to learn profound
meditation Bukko

If you walk, walk!
If you sit, sit!
Just don't wobble
whatever you do!
Ummon

"What is the Truth?" the monk asked
"Here I sit on Daigu Peak!"
Hyakujo answered

The disciple asked:
- What is the Buddha's opinion in this matter?
The Buddha answered:
- The Buddha does not hold opinions.

If Christ were born
a thousand times
in Galilee
it was all in vain
until he is born in thee,
in me

Angelus Silesius

I set out to beg
my food
but spent my time
gathering violets
in the fields of Spring

Ryokan

the existent
and the non existent
are the same under
different names
Lao Tzu

the Void is a living Void

pulsating in endless rhythms of creation and destruction. The great Void does not exist as Void, it embraces all Being / non-Being

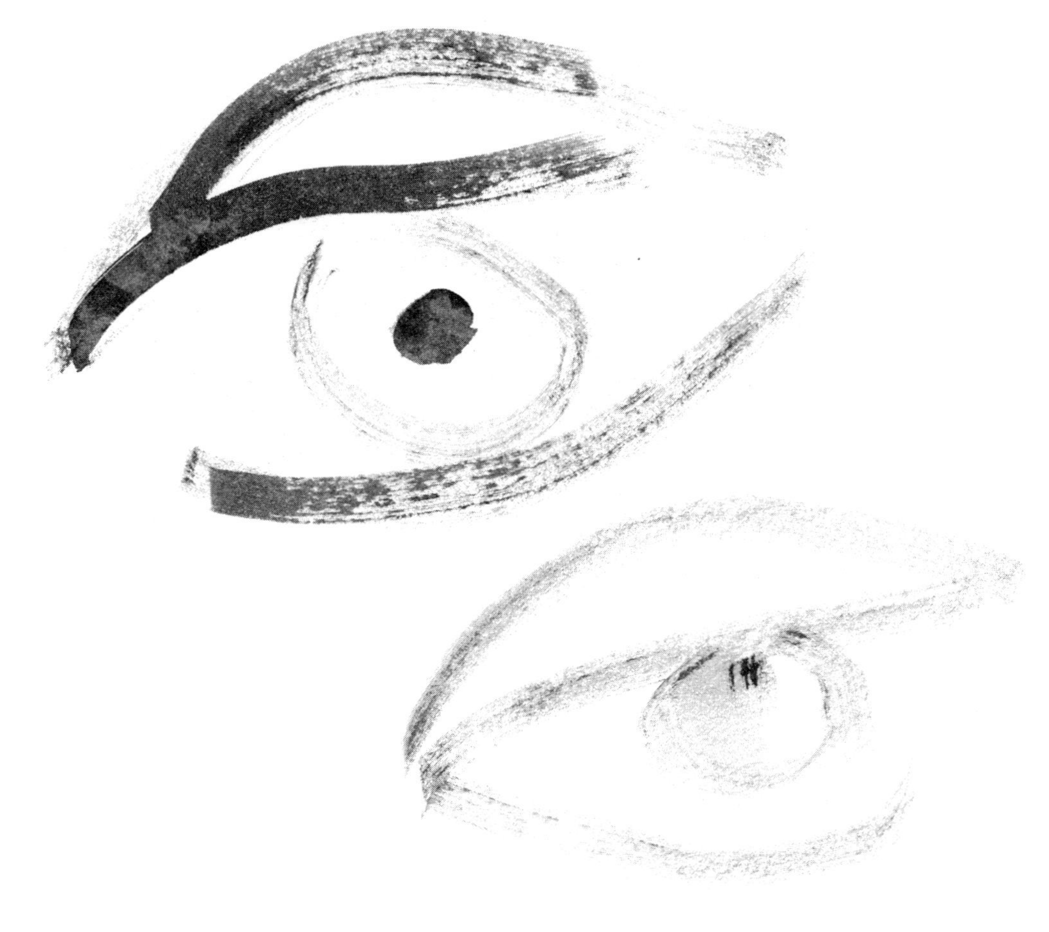

The eye with which I see
God
is the same Eye with which
God
sees me

Meister Eckhart

Do you believe in God?

I? I believe in nothing but God!"

Why doest thou prate of God?

Whatever thou sayest is untrue . . .

Meister Eckhart

"Do you believe in God?"
"Which one?"

Anyone who pretends
he Knows God is depraved

St. Gregory Nanzianzen

if you say
"God exists"
then act
as if
God exists.

Nietzsche killed God
and went mad...

The Buddha
did the same
and attained
Ultimate
Sanity

God is no uncle, God is an Earthquake!

Hassidic saying

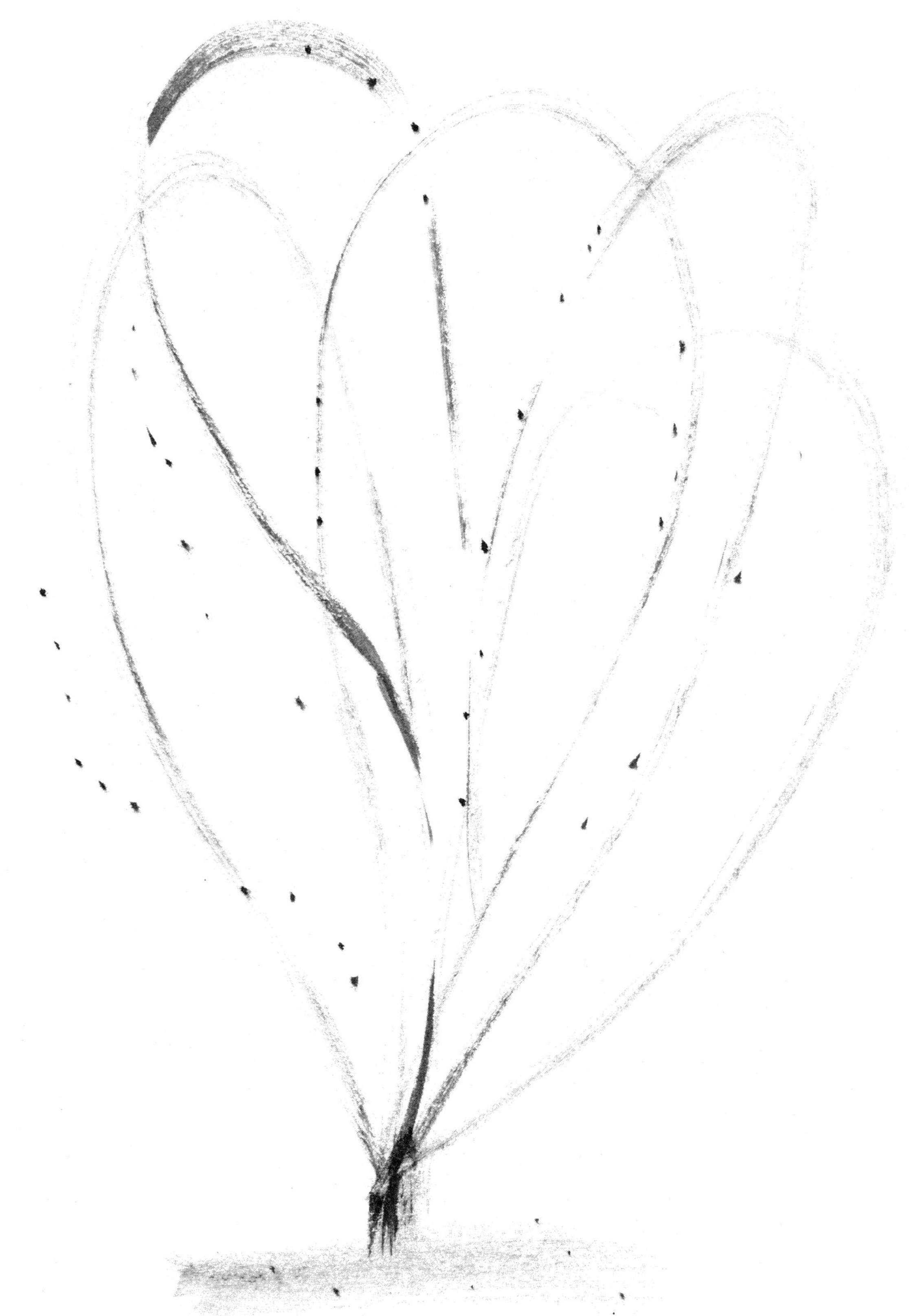

God is a fountain flowing into Itself

Dionysius

Spiritual talk
makes a fine cover
to sell a lie . . .

The religions are
delusional constructs
formed around
an infallible core

Quite
apart
from religion:
there are
the plumblossoms,
the apple blossoms
nanpoku

ask!
knock!

but don't let anyone
sell you anything...

for
– Your treasure house is within,
it contains all you'll ever need
Hui Hai

It is not that things are delusory
but their separateness in the fabric
of the Whole that is illusory...

At first the mountains
are mountains,
then the mountain are
mountains no longer
until finally the mountains are mountains indeed.

When the mountains are
no longer mountains
is it because
I
am no longer
I ?

Heaven and Earth are of one root
the Ten Thousand Things
and I
are of one body

Zazenron

Solitary
body
in
the
midst
of
the Ten Thousand
things...

Keiji Nishitani

people walking?

Karma walking...

Buddha Nature walking..!

Zuizan used to call out to himself:

- Zuizan!
- Yes, Master, he answered
- Are you awake?
- Yes, Master!
- Really awake?
- Oh, yes, Master!!
- And won't you let yourself be deceived again?
- No, Master! Never!

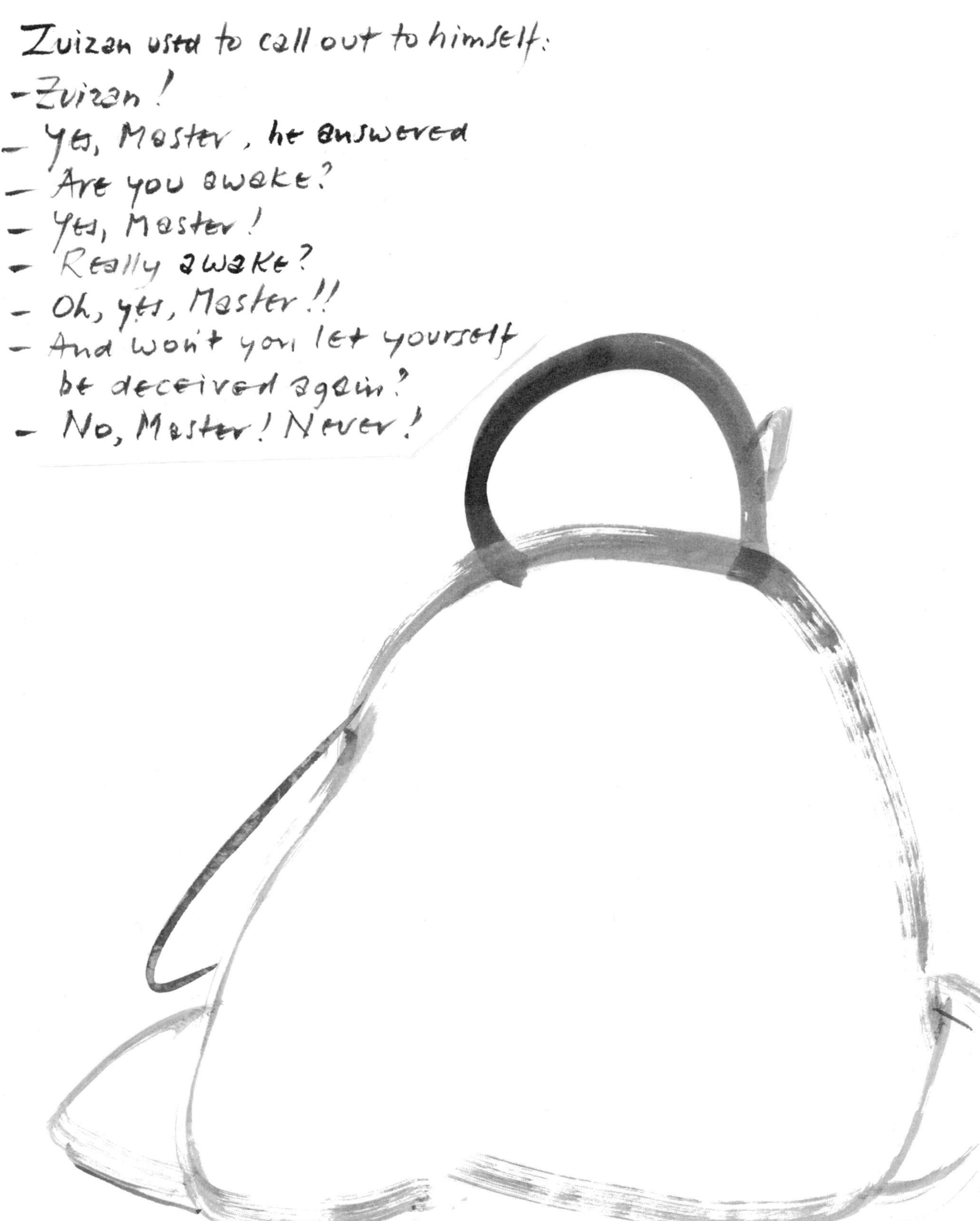

Holy?
nothing holy, Your Majesty!
all holy! Great Emptiness!

Bodhidharma

Who are you?
I do not know, Your Majesty...

Bodhidharma

how well it explains the
truth, the Buddha,
how profoundly it speaks
of the true nature of
things, the swallow!

Issa

"All the mountains, rivers, this whole great earth,
where does it come from?" the monk asked.
The Master answered: "Where does your question come from"

the real tree as it stands there
Stands before the eye as
growing from the depth of
Nothingness

Prajna Paramita Sutra

If you still have to talk
about Ultimate Reality
see how it manifests Itself
nakedly
in
every thing!

What is the Buddha? the monk asked
The oak tree in the front yard! Joshu replied

The perceptible is No Thingness... No Thingness
is no other than the perceptible

Prajna Paramita Sutra

When the Ten Thousand Things are seen in their Oneness,
we return to the Origins and remain where we have always been.
Seng T'sen

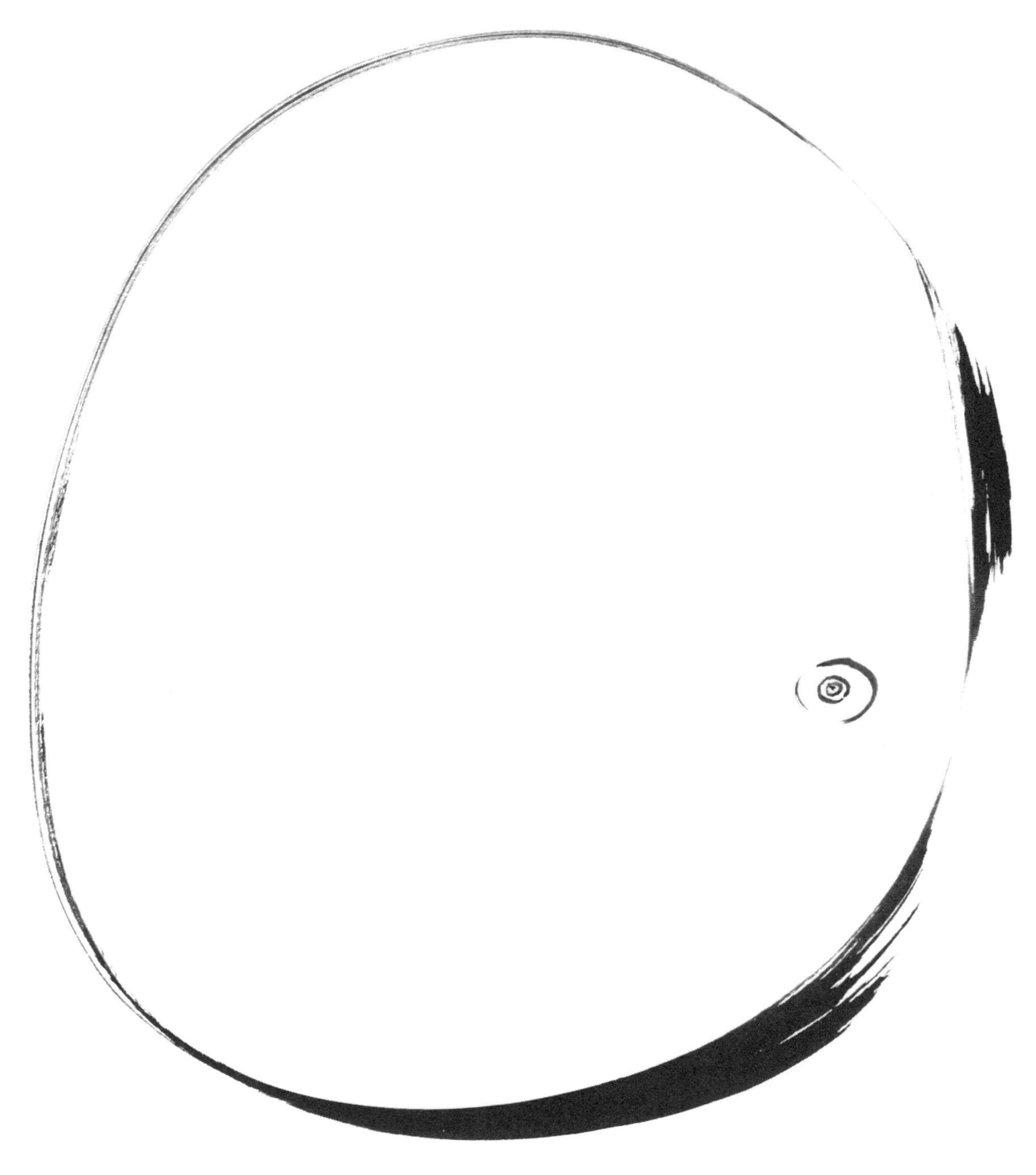

In the beginningless beginning
there was
the Meaning . . .

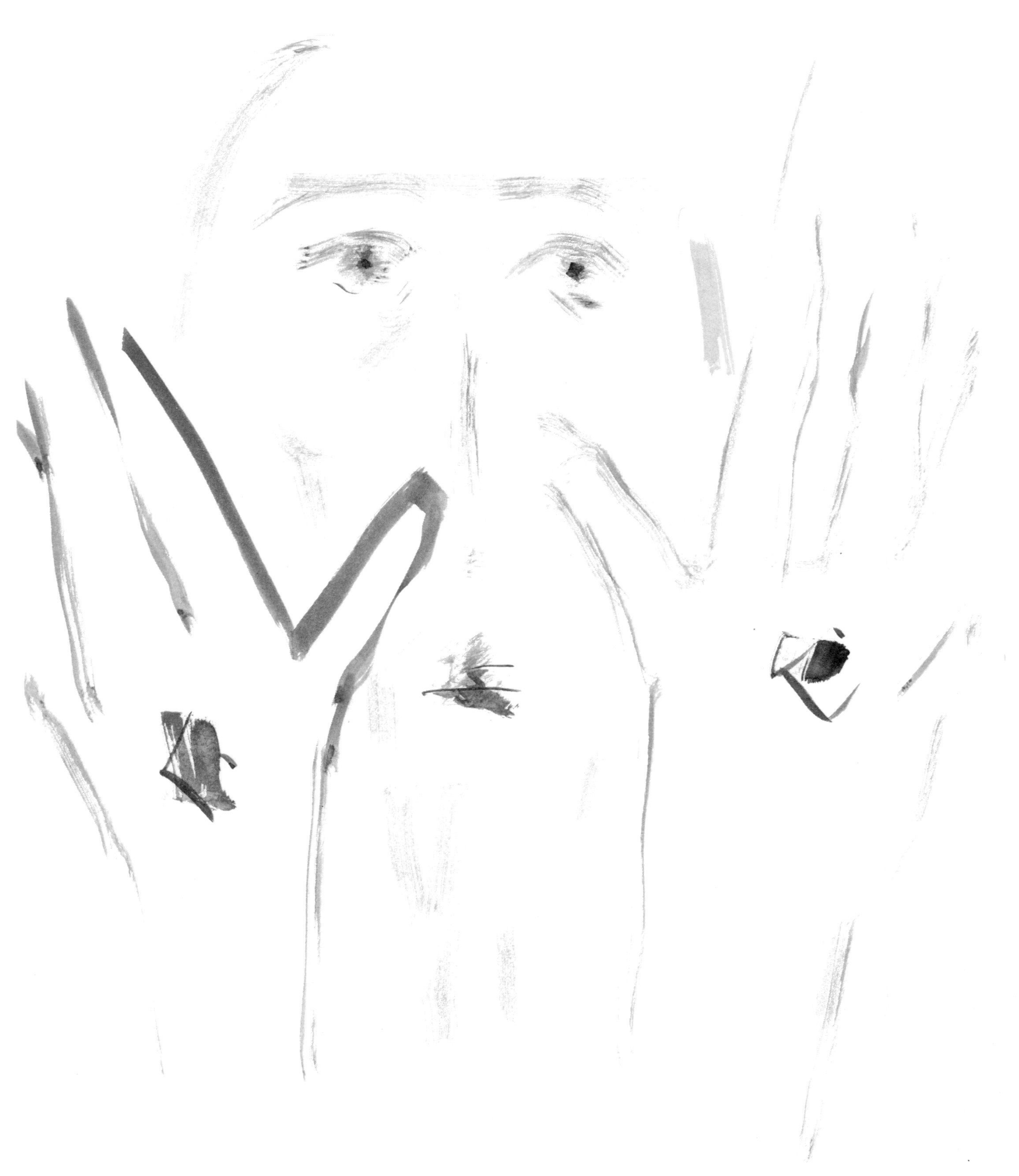

Emmaus: Who has seen Me has seen the Real

When the Christ says I:
it is the I of all the Masters:
the Way, the Truth,
the Life

I and the Father are not-two!

In the beginning
was the Word.
behold the One
to Whom Mary listened

and the Word
was made flesh,
behold the One
whom Martha served

St Augustine

the Kingdom is within you
and without you

gospel acc. to Thomas

the grasses
whisper

"This
is
my
Body"

this is my Body

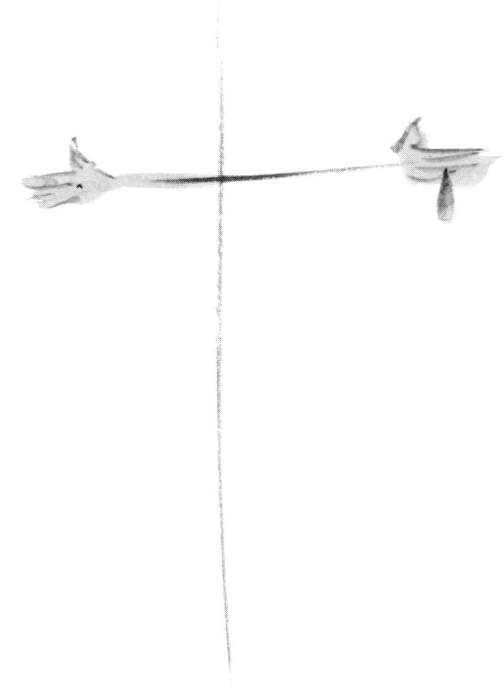

The Christ has no body on earth, no hands, no feet
but yours... Theresa of Avila

This
is
My
body

Innumerable Buddhas
Enlightened...
innumerable Christs crucified...
always the same Christ, the same Buddha!

CHRIST NATURE <u>IS</u>!

BUDDHA NATURE <u>IS</u>!

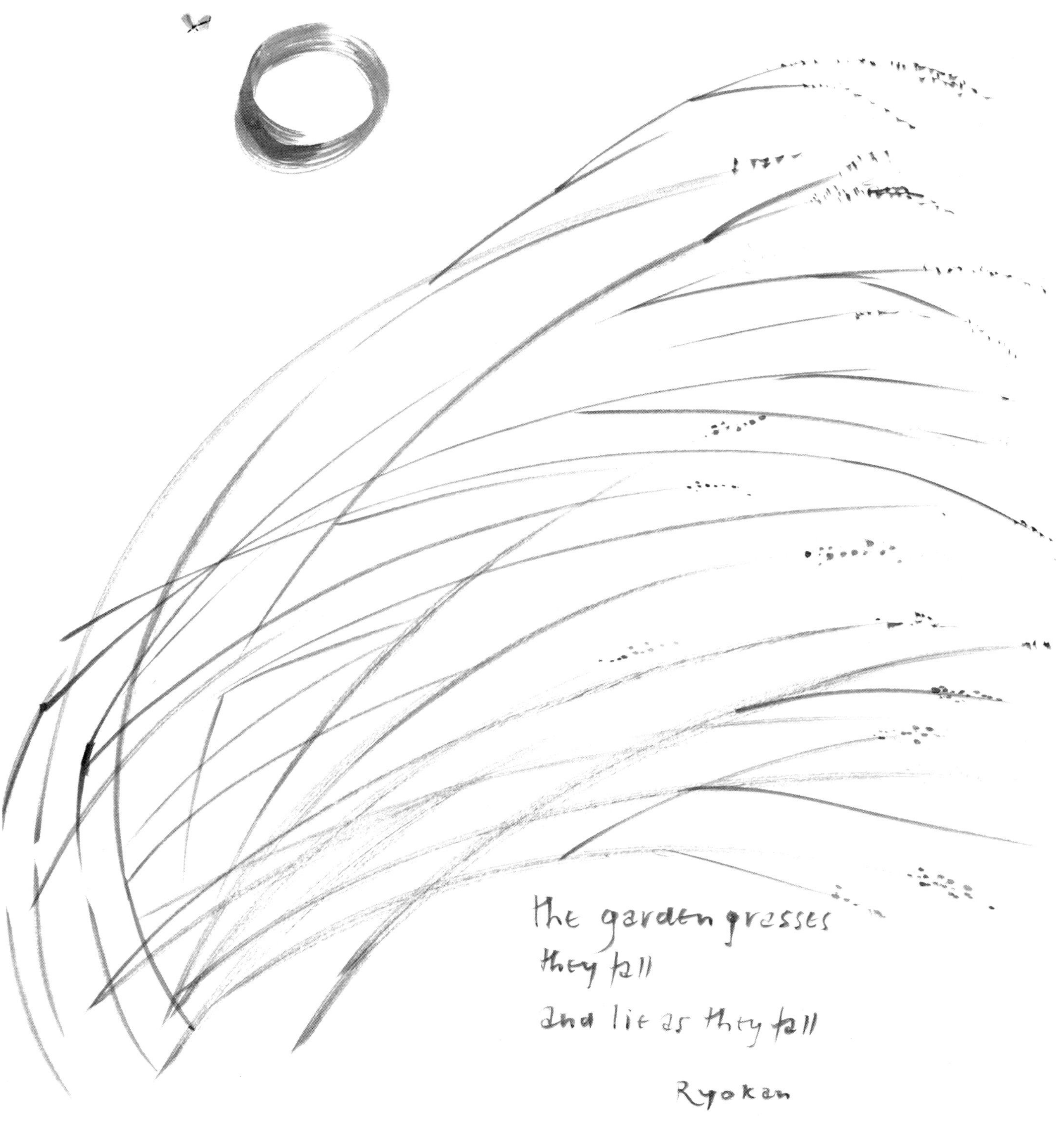
the garden grasses
they fall
and lie as they fall
Ryokan

What dwelleth here
I know not
but my heart is
full of awe
and the tears trickle down
Saicho

"I saw you planting trees today deep in the mountains. Why?"

"Will they not be a lovely sight from here when they grow tall? Will they not be a delight for future generations?" the Master answered.

In my hut
this spring
there is nothing
there is Everything

It is deep autumn
What kind of life
is my neighbor's,
I wonder
Basho

the Noumenon expresses Itself ceaselessly in the phenomena

Sitting quietly
spring comes
the grass grows
by itself
zenrin

if a man sees the Tao
in the morning

he may die in the evening
regretting nothing

Confucius

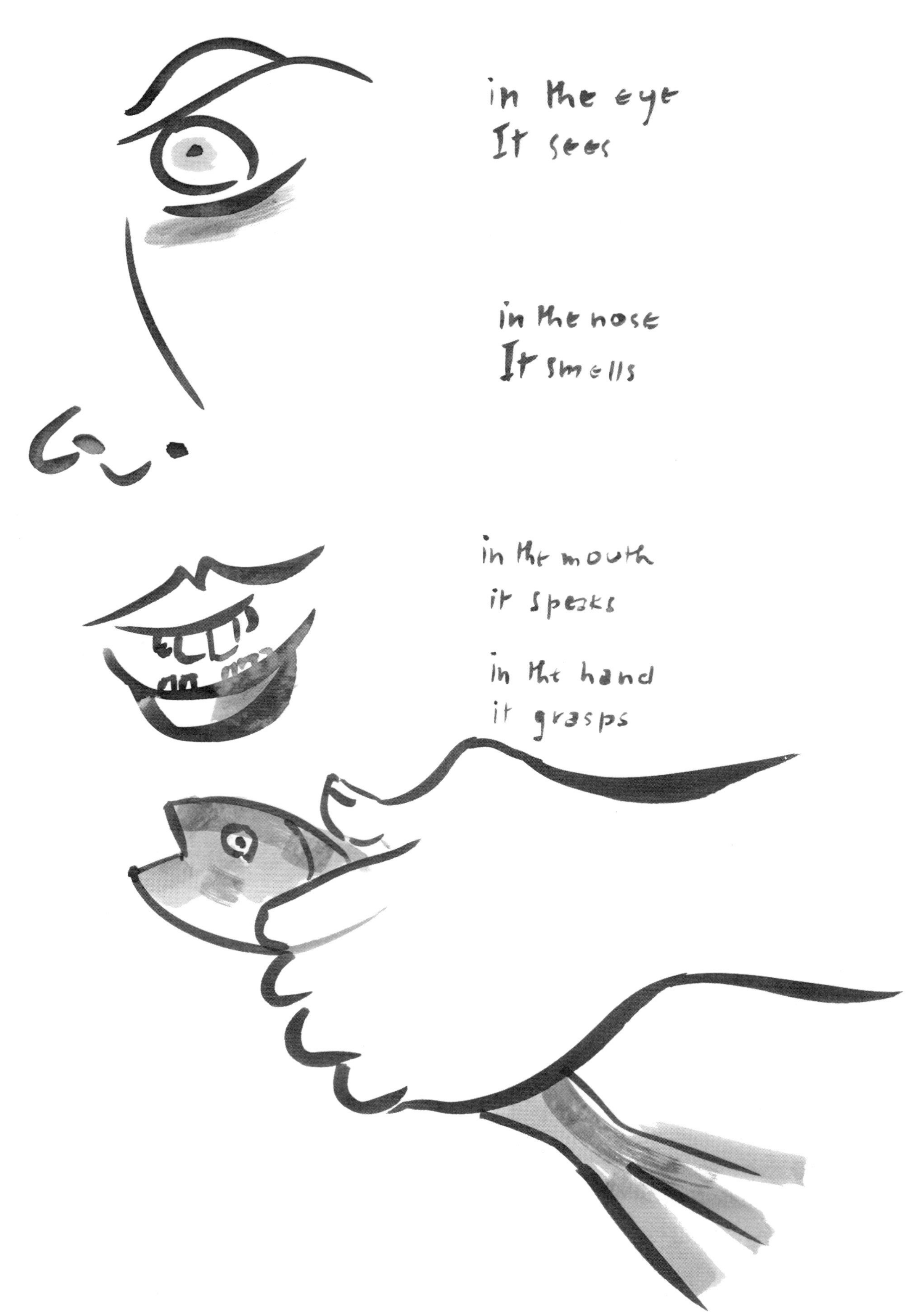
in the eye
It sees
in the nose
It smells
in the mouth
it speaks
in the hand
it grasps

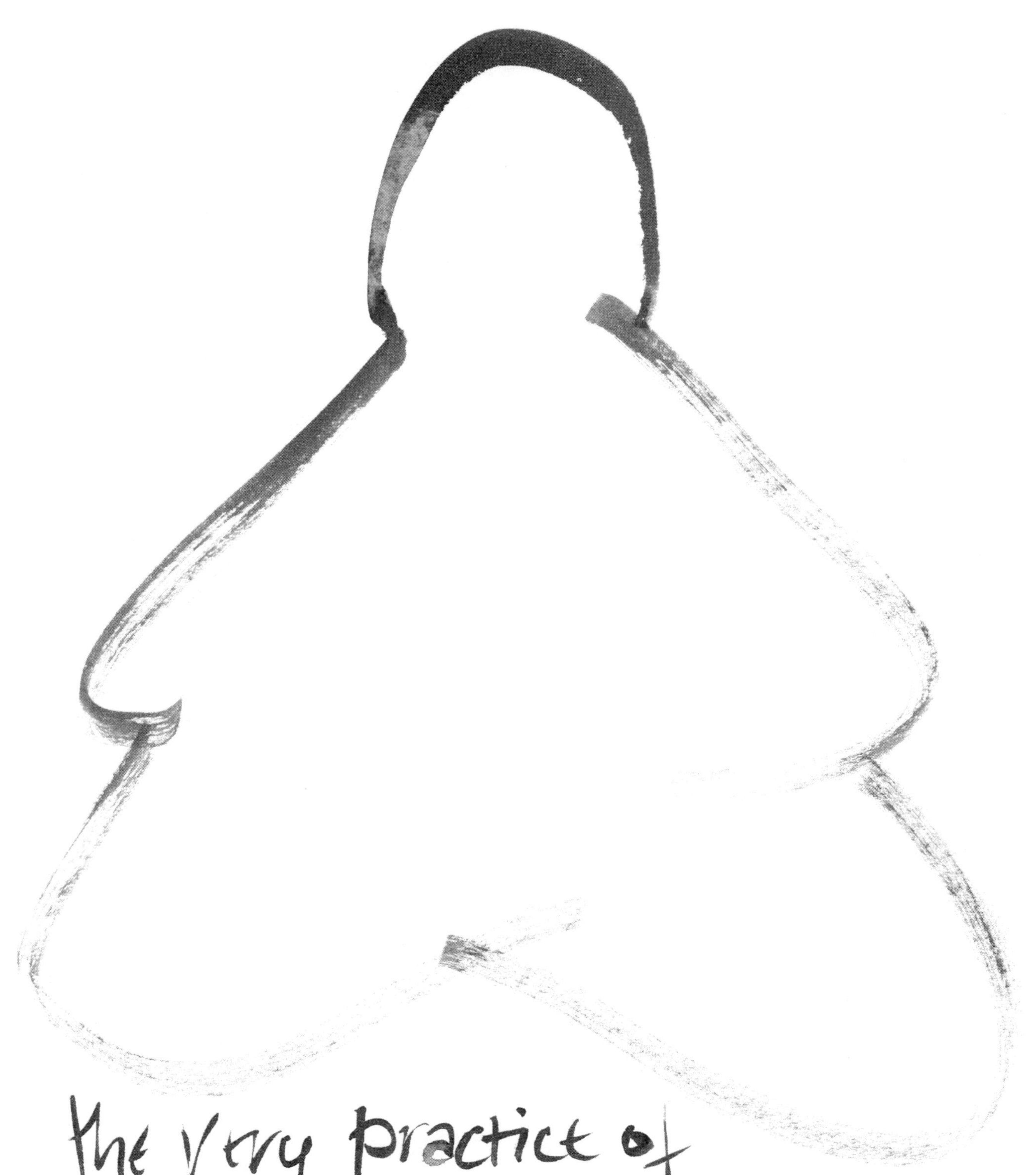

the very practice of
the Buddha — this is the Buddha!

Hui Neng

He who seeks the Buddha
outside of his own mind
makes the Buddha
into a devil
Dogen

Become angry and you turn the Buddha Mind into a Fighting Demon—vent your selfishness and you turn it into a Hungry Ghost, give free rein to your folly and you make it into an animal!

Bankei

Both the slayer
and the slain
are like dewdrops
thus to be regarded

Neither the wind!
nor the flag!
It is your mind
that is blowing
Nansen

Summer grasses
all that remains
of the warrior's
dream

Just as there are those
who attain Enlightenment
beyond Enlightenment
there are those who fall
into delusion beyond
delusion...

Dogen

"Nothing burns in hell but ego" says Tauler.
Does anything live on but Buddha Nature, Christ Spirit?

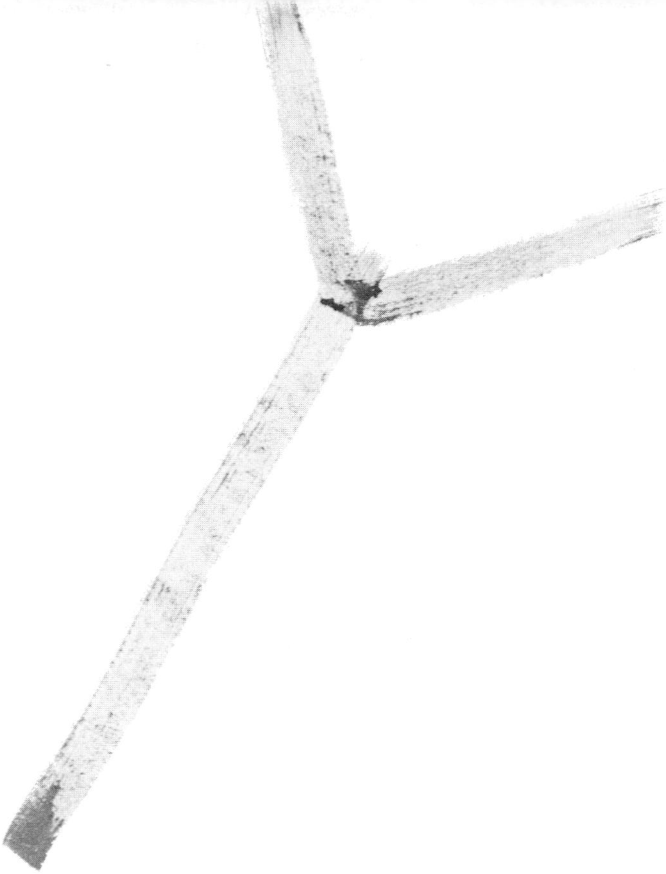

the cross
of the Crucifixion—
without
the cross
of the Resurrection
is the symbol
of a
mutilated
Christianity

Even ghosts will
attain
enlightenment...
Lankavatara
Sutra

they have taken the wounds of
the people lightly.. they say
peace, peace, where there is
no peace...
Jeremiah 6.14

they do not see what they look at,

hence they know not what they do

When this is realized the Great Compassion arises:
"May all beings be fulfilled!"

See how it
wrings its hands
and feet
the fly
oh kill it not

Issa

I will not let thee go
unless Thou blesseth me!

Genesis XXXII

I am come as Time,
the waster of peoples
ready for the hour
that ripens their ruin

Upanishads

Let there be Light!
He said.

Who was the eyewitness?

Let there be dark!
We said

Who will be the eyewitness?

Where did the dead monk go?
he asked

Seppo said:
It was like ice becoming water...

Gensha objected:
No, it's like water
returning to water!

sentient beings are
intrinsically Buddhas
It is like water and ice
without water ice can't exist

Hakuin

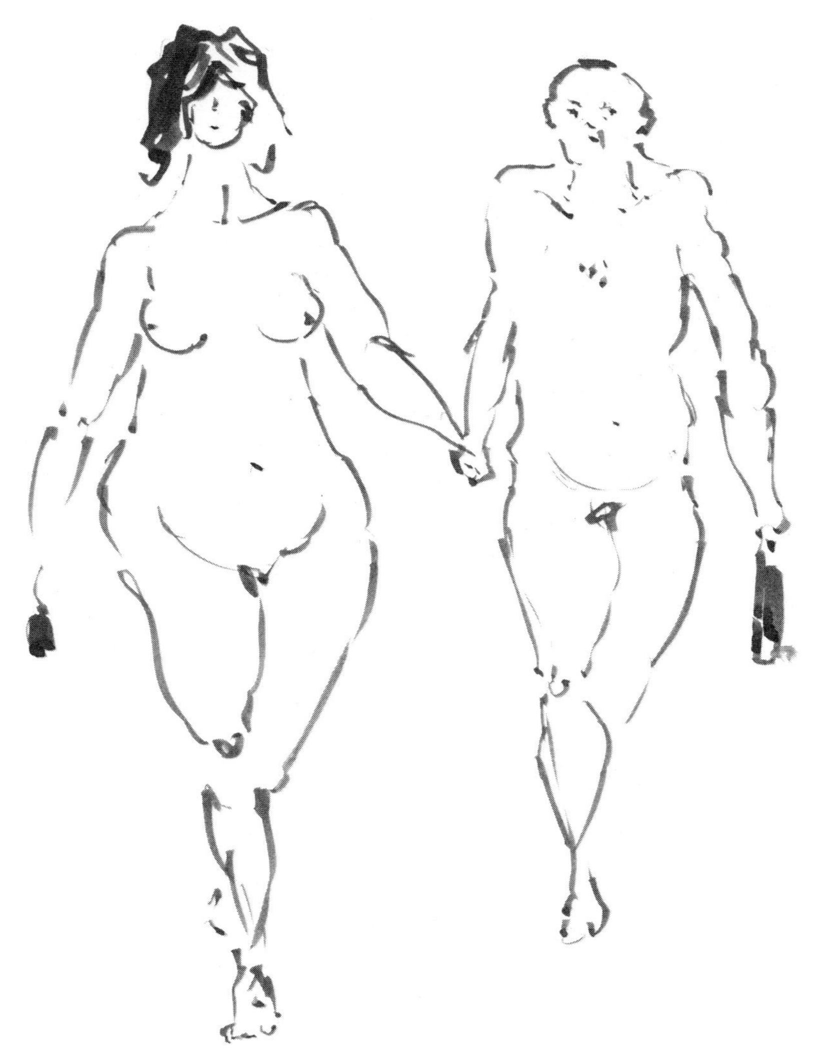

If you want to do
a certain thing
you first have to become
a certain person

once you have become
that certain person
you will not care
anymore about
doing that certain thing

Dogen

There was a fisherman in China who sat fishing with a straight needle, year after year. People wondered and talked about this strange fisherman until the story reached the Emperor, who decided to take a look at this phenomenon in person.
– Now tell me, my good man, what do you hope to catch with that straight needle? And the man answered: – You, your Majesty!

the nightingale
even before His Lordship
the same voice

Issa

parted eons ago

yet never separated
for a moment.

Daito

"What's your name? Enen asked Ejaku?
My name is Enen! said Ejaku
But Enen, that's my name!!
O.K, said Ejaku, in that case I'm Ejaku..!
and they roared with laughter.

the distance
between this pigeon's brain
and mine
is minute
compared to that
between mine
and Bodhi's
Wisdom
Compassion

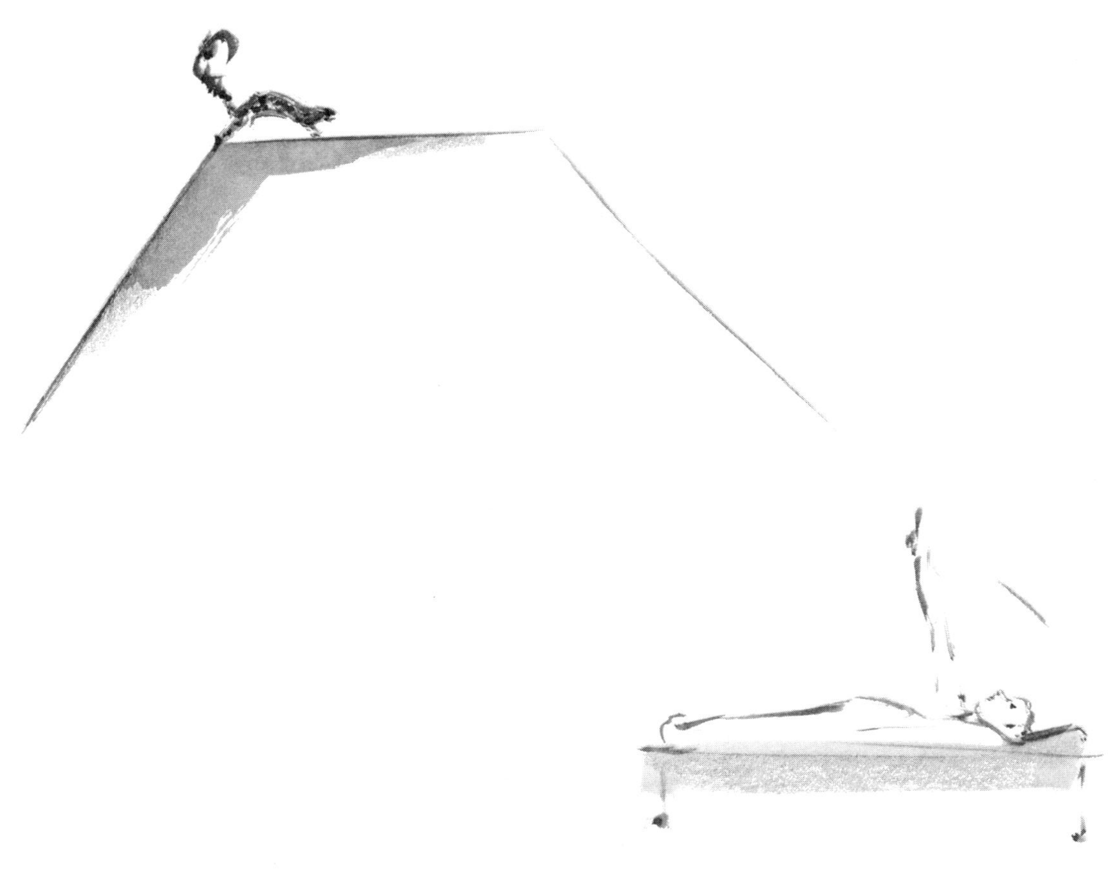

When Kukai lay dying, he heard
a squirrel screeching on the roof.
He bid his disciples listen.
–This is It, he said, and nothing more!

Where does the soul go
when the body dies?
It does not need to go
anywhere.

Jakob Boehme

I came alone

I'll die alone

in between times
I'm just alone
day and night

Sengai

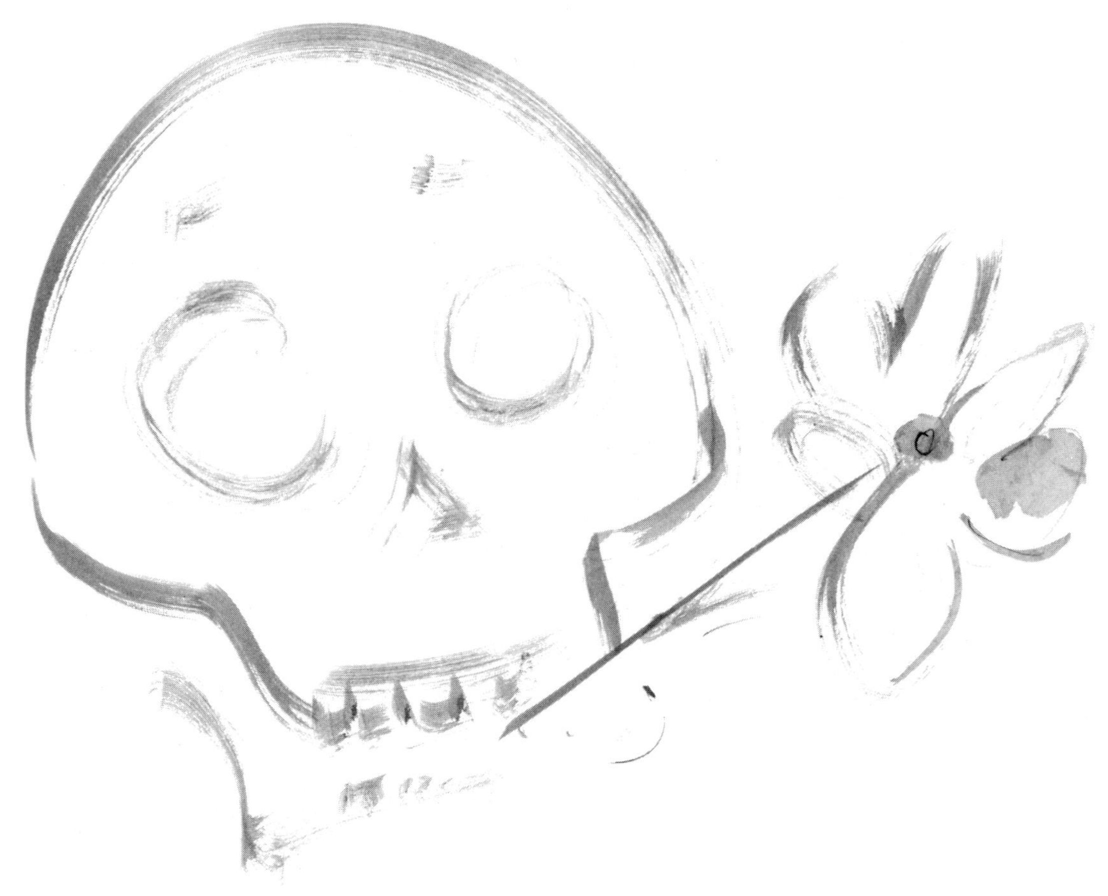

I shall not die
I shall not go anywhere
just dont ask me
any questions.
I shall not answer

Ikkyu

What do I bequeathe
as my legacy:
flowers of spring
cuckoos in summer
maple leaves of autumn
Ryokan

life ends with the previous thought

it is resuscitated with the subsequent one

"He who knows speaks not," said Lao Tze

"If he knew... then why did he write those 5000 words?"

Hakurakuten

"Why does a cow give milk?"
"Ask her!"

don't dismiss these
as verses
an old fellow
likes to scribble!
What I have in mind
is to arouse,
to open someone's eye
here or there.
The bright one will
see at a glance where
the arrow flies,
the dull will prattle
about rhythm
and rhyme.

Hakuin

FREDERICK FRANCK, whose drawings and paintings are part of the permanent collections of a score of museums in America and abroad, including the Museum of Modern Art, the Whitney Museum, the Fogg Museum and the Tokyo National Museum, is an uncommonly versatile man. He holds degrees in Medicine, Dentistry, and Fine Arts. For three years he served on the staff of Dr. Albert Schweitzer at Lambaréné. He was the only artist to record all four sessions of the Second Vatican Council (1962-1965).

His many books deal with Africa and Albert Schweitzer, with religious experience, and with his concept of drawing. In his best known book, "The Zen of Seeing," he speaks of drawing as a spiritual discipline, an equivalent of meditation and prayer.

In memory of Pope John XXIII, for whom he has unbounded admiration, he converted the ruins of an eighteenth-century watermill near his house in Warwick N.Y., into "PACEM in TERRIS," a "trans-religious oasis of inwardness." Among the artistic and spiritual events at "Pacem in Terris" are workshops on "seeing/drawing as meditation," and performances of Franck's own contemporary version of the medieval Play of Everyman.